Whisky & Beards Publishing

WhiskyandBeards.co.uk

Hags Ahoy

HagsAhoy.com

ISBN: 978-1-9160962-0-2

Right of Entitlement

by Steven Todd

The stage is set with two chairs and a small table. There is low, neutral lighting which comes up as the actors take the stage.

Together: Two persons, one room.
He must find the key to she.
She does not see there is a key

Jacob: Quid est forsit eius?

Cleo: He asks

Jacob is sitting, Cleo is standing with her back to him, looking at some framed qualifications which are on the 4th wall.

J: Can I get you a drink? Tea, coffee, water? I could send out for squash?

C: (*Looks expressionlessly at him, then back to the wall*) These all yours?

J: Yes

C: Your parents must have been really rich.

J: They didn't buy them.

C: No. (*She points at one*) Glasgow.

J: I studied history there.

C: (*Looks at him*) Your parents must have been really rich.

J: What, Glasgow? Besides, I got a grant. You could still get grants in those days.

C: So you went back and did psychology?

J: After my Masters. I mastered in psychology at Birkbeck, then went to the institute of psychiatry.

C: The institute of psychiatry? Nice.

J: Or to give it its full title, the institute of psychiatry, psychology and neuroscience. IOPPN.

C: Eye open?

J: It's an acronym, IOPPN. Stands for the institute of psychiatry, psychology and so on. Though, to be honest, it was just the institute of psychiatry in my day.

C: Bet it was excellent.

J: It was, yes. Still is. It works in tandem with the South London and Maudsley NHS foundation trust. Some of the senior staff are consultants there.

C: And how long did all this take?

J: About a decade.

C: And did you get a grant for that as well?

J: A small one. My parents helped me out.

C: (*Shakes her head*)

J: And I worked. (*Pause*)

J: So....what's the relationship with your parents like?

C: I'm their daughter.

J: So they're still together?

C: Says so in my notes, doesn't it?

J: Probably. I prefer to meet a person before reading everything about them. Talk.

C: Nice.

J: Do you get on with them?

C: Very well.

J: Very well? OK. And, are you an only child?

C: No. I have a brother.

J: Older or younger?

C: Is it relevant?

J: It could be.

C: Then he's younger.

J: He....is younger.

C: Not going to get far if I have to validate everything I say.

J: No.

C: (*points at qualification*) Did you meet your wife there?

J: At the institute? As a matter of fact I did. Good guess.

C: It wasn't a guess. (*pause*) What's her name?

J: Susan.

C: She do this too?

J: Used to. She stopped when we had Archie, and somehow never...runs her own business now.

C: Your son's name is Archie? Like Robot Archie?

J: I would have thought you'd be a little young to know about Robot Archie. He's from before my time.

C: But you know who he is. (*pause*) Archie. Not a very nice name to give a kid.

J: Archie's 23.

C: Yeah, but he wasn't always. Once he was 11, just starting at big school, where some of the other kids would smirk and look at each other.

J: It wasn't like that!

C: You were there? (*pause*)

J: Is that what it's like for you? I mean, Cleo....quite an unusual name. Do you get picked on at all?

C: No. Not at all. Most of the kids like it.

J: (*leafing through her notes*) You were born in Poland.

C: I know.

J: I'm just looking at your notes. Not a very Polish name, though, Cleo.

C: My mum was a big fan of Cleo Lane.

J: OK. The jazz singer. So how do you feel you've settled here?

C: I've been here most of my life. What do you think?

J: Yes, but I can still trace an accent.

C: Both of my parents are Polish.

J: OK. And how would you say they'd settled?

C: Brilliantly. We've all settled brilliantly Everything is brilliant.

J: OK.

C: Is that yours?

J: The CD? Yeah.

C: The Zutons?

J: Do you know them?

C: Yes. They wrote Valerie. They're dreadful.

J: Do you prefer the Amy Winehouse version?

C: No. It's a dreadful song.

J: Right. So what kind of stuff do you prefer? Rap, R'n'B?

C: R'n'B? You mean like Bo Diddley?

J: Do your parents like Bo Diddley too?

C: No. Don't suppose they've ever heard of him.

J: I'm surprised you have. I mean, he is from the 50s.

C: And the 60s. In fact he didn't die until 2008.

J: So you like old blues guys?

C: Not particularly. But they're good. Unlike the Zutons.

J: OK.

C: I'm glad it's OK. Now are you going to ask me about the graffiti? I mean, that's why I'm here, isn't it?

J: Just thought we could chat a little first.

C: Alright. We'll 'chat'. Where did you work?

J: When?

C: When you were at the 'eye open'. You said you got a small grant, your parents helped you out, and you worked.

J: Oh. Right. In a record shop. A second hand record shop, part time.

C: (*nodding*) Part time. And was it fun?

J: Yes, mostly.(*chuckles to himself*)I remember one time a chap came in with an LP he'd bought a few days earlier. Called Surfin with Bo Diddley. Wanted his money back. I said, 'What's wrong with it?' He said, 'There's no Diddley. (He laughs. She doesn't)

J: Which was true. It wasn't really a Bo Diddley record at all. Just a lot of duff instrumentals. I remember Bo himself doing an awful version of Old Man River, of all things.

C: I thought there was no Diddley.

J: Well....there wasn't much Diddley. Little bit of Diddley. I believe it was mostly a chap called Billy Lee Riley.

C: Flying Saucers Rock and Roll.

J: You know him?

C: Not personally. Does 'Susan' like music?

J: Very much. Well, she doesn't seem to listen to so much nowadays.

C: Law of evolution. Jacob looks puzzled.

C: People stop doing things as they get older. Eventually they refine it to just drinking and watching telly.

(*The lighting takes on a blue tinge*)

J: OK. How many words can you give me beginning with....J

C: Aha! The tests begin.

(*Silence while he looks at her expectantly*)

C: Judge. Jury. Jurisdiction. Gerrymandering, which actually begins with a G, but it's a good word. And Juno, which is a film.

J: Any more?

C: How many would you like? (*He shrugs*)

C: Juice. Jack. Jackboot. Jack shit. Jack of all trades, jack it all in. Jersey, which could also be a place, but that too would begin with a G, and be a lot less relevant. And....jockstrap.

J: A lot less relevant than what?

(*She doesn't answer*)

J: A lot less relevant than gerrymandering? Is that what you meant?

C: (shrugs)

J: You said Jersey, which could also be a place, but that too would begin with a G and be a lot less relevant. Do you actually know what gerrymandering means?

C: Of course.

J: Why 'of course'? You seem to think that the isle of Jersey begins with a G, which it doesn't. I think you're thinking of Guernsey, which is another of the channel islands. So we aren't always right with things we think we know. So, given that, are you sure you know what gerrymandering means?

C: (stares at him right in the eyes) It means to manipulate things in favour of one class.

J: Really?

C: (*shrugs and turns away*)

J: Well, you're not entirely wrong. It means to manipulate boundaries in favour of one class. Or party. It's an election thing. Refers to elections.

(*Silence*)

J: "Ruthless is clean, unknowing the naked bones of heaven." What does that mean?

C: In general, or to me?

J: To you. You wrote it.

C: I didn't write it. I recreated it.

J: That's semantics. You painted those words on the south wall of the westward track at Paddington station, in white letters, each one exactly 18 inches high. So what does it mean?

C: You can't just say.

J: Why not? What do you have to do first?

C: You have to think about it.

J: I think you've had sufficient time to think about it.

C: What does it suggest to you?

J: I'm asking you that.

C: No, you're asking me what it means. I'm trying to put you in the right mindset to get it.

J: What's to get?

C: What comes into your mind when you hear those words?

J: What are the naked bones of heaven?

C: (*Rolls her eyes*) What does it suggest?

J: (*Ponders*) Ruthless is clean....ruthless is clean unknowing...er....no knowledge, with which to ameliorate, or...to improve the situation? I suppose, hence ruthless. The naked bones of heaven. Heaven scaled back? Heaven in the raw? Raw heaven? No knowledge of raw heaven?

C: That’s what it suggests to you, does it? No knowledge of raw heaven?

J: (*embarrassed*) Well, that’s just…

C: No, that’s good, really. At least you gave it ten seconds thought, which is more than anyone else has so far. Everyone else is convinced I was just mashed off my tits at the time.

J: And you weren’t?

C: No.

J: OK. Do you use drugs at all?

C: No.

J: Really?

C: Yes, really. Amazing, isn’t it? A young person that doesn't take drugs? What are you going to do without that stereotype?

(*pause*)

J: Look, I’m going to try something, so bear with me. I’m going to say a word, and I want you to reply with the first word that enters your head. OK?

C: Of course.

J: Alright, er, right.....sandwich.

C: Tea break.

J: Canteen

C: Chocolate.

J: Sugar

C: Diet

J: Wait a moment. Sorry, it’s my fault. I didn’t get breakfast this morning. I think my stomach suggested that one.

C: Get something to eat. I don’t mind.

J: No, it’s not long till lunch now. OK....light.

C: Spirit

J: Drink

C: Bar

J: Veto

C: Drink

J: Spir...no, wait

C: Would you like a drink as well?

J: Ready? Persist.

C: Hair clip.

J: (*Raises an eyebrow*) Brush

C: Fox

J: Tail

C: Detective

J: Gangster

C: Cinema

J: Darkness

C: Bridge

J: Span

C: Sink

J: Eddy

C: (*pause*) I'm not going to say drown, if that's what you're waiting for.

J: I wasn't waiting for anything. (*pause*) Ready to go again?

C: Your house, your rules.

J: My office.

C: (*shrugs*)

J: Spring

C: Pounce

J: Capture

C: Ransom

J: Freedom

C: Library

J: (*nodding*) Knowledge

C: Entrapment.

(*Silence*)

C: And?

J: Sorry, I was just considering something.

C: Shall I come back another time?

J: Could I just do a little test on you?

C: A little test?

J: Well...all you have to do is pick your three favourite animals. One, two, three. Then say something about each of them. As much as you like.

C: Now?

J: Yes.

C: Can I have a moment to think about it?

J: Of course, would you like something to drink while you're thinking?

C: No. Thank you.(*pause*)

J: Why did you think the word gerrymandering was so relevant?

C: Why do you think?

J: I'm guessing you feel things are slanted in favour of the middle classes.

C: And they're not?

J: You like to answer questions with questions, don't you?

C: He asks!

J: Touché.

C: It's Socratic.

J: Socratic? Impressive. Socratic debate. A form of argumentative dialogue based upon the asking and answering of questions to stimulate critical thinking.

C: (*pause*) And?

J: Was that quote on the wall....was that a kind of question? I mean....were you…

C: Asking a question?

J: Yes?

C: Yes.

J: And what was the question?

C: You want everything spelled out, don't you?

J: Ideally, yes.

C: You put a quote on a wall, one that no one's expecting, one that doesn't appear to make sense, but if it's there long enough - and if you pick the right spot, it will be - it will eventually cause people to ponder, wonder about it. At least be surprised.

J: So that was your sole intention? To make people wonder?

C: No. But what if it was? Is that such a bad thing? I mean every Christmas when you used to produce presents for little Archie, didn't it make you feel good to see his eyes fill with wonder? When did your eyes last fill with wonder?

J: Come on. Aren't you conflating two separate meanings here? Yes, wonder can mean amazement at some beautiful object or thing; but it can also mean just to be curious.

C: Yes, and which of those is the undesirable one?

J: Fine. So people are curious about this....this question you're asking. And they ponder it. Why should they be surprised?

(*She looks at him*)

J: You said, they might at least be surprised. You mean, at the oddness of the quote?

C: How much graffiti have you seen?

J: Quite a lot. It is everywhere.

C: And what have you noticed about it?

J: Apart from its being rather irritating, you mean?

C: Yes.

J: It's childish. It's ugly, it spoils buildings, walls, doesn't speak outside of its little clique, for a start.

C: It's reversed appropriation.

J: What do you mean by that?

C: I meant reversed cultural appropriation.

J: I still don't follow.

C: You've been to our school, you've seen a lot of the people I go to school with. Few Eastern Europeans like myself, few Caribbeans. Loads of kids from round here or wherever, but no Americans that I know of, yet it's all gangs, funky ass trainers, baseball caps, rap. They've got no identity of their own. They go crawling up a tower after school, or across several railway lines, risking their necks just to write toxo or something on a wall.

J: Yes. It's called tagging. They want their names to be seen, their symbols. And the repeated use of the symbols marks their territory. They think it shows courage, resourcefulness, a blindness to the rules. What you did was basically tagging.

C: How was it? I wrote something more than just a stupid symbol. It was only by chance anyone found out it was me. I certainly didn't mean them to. These idiots I'm talking about make a big show of having nothing to say.

J: But you still risked your neck putting it there. You do realise three people were killed doing just that this past month.

(*long pause*)

C: Where?

J: On an elevated section of track, somewhere between Brixton and Denmark Hill. The Police found all their equipment, spray cans and so forth, by the bodies.

C: How old were they?

J: Older than you. One was 19, the other two I think in their early 20s. Actually the youngest boy was American. And there was some controversy because a man called Brian Cook took exception to the BBC referring to them as graffiti artists, and tweeted that they were nothing but common scum.

C: Wow. Empathy. Tory MP?

J: Not quite. He was Chairman of the Beckenham Conservative association, I think. Whatever, he got himself suspended anyway.

C: Good.

J: So what did you mean by reversed cultural appropriation? You think they're appropriating Black American culture, or something?

C: My father was 10 years old when his uncle took him to New York. That's where he saw hip-hop graffiti for the first time. It was exactly the same then as it is now. Same colouring, same bubble lettering, nothing added. I should have said generational appropriation.

J: Well, that's a new one.

C: How old are you?

J: (*coyly*) Late 50s.

C: So you were about 20 in the late 70s?

J: Yes, roughly.

C: Well, that's when my dad was in New York, when you were about 20. Nearly 40 years ago. What were you doing then? I bet you weren't listening to Vera Lynn.

J: Why would I be?

C: Because that's what you'd have to have been doing, to copy what people were doing 40 years before. You'd have to go back to the second world war. Time has stood still for my generation. The only change is we get to put our emptiness out on social media.

J: That's an interesting point. Never thought of it that way.

C: Nobody does.

J: You use social media?

C: Everybody of my generation uses social media. We're a generation marked out by the quickness of our thumbs and the dryness of our eyes. Or whatever other horrific side-effects there might be from growing up staring at screens.

J: You're an odd girl. You claim to be happy at school and happy at home, yet, if you don't mind my saying so, you display a pretty high level of discontent.

C: Ruthless is clean unknowing the naked bones of heaven.

J: OK, so you've obviously put a lot of thought into that quote. Where does it come from?

C: Thought you'd have googled it.

J: I did. I couldn't find it.(pause) There were a couple of references to a song called Busy Drowning. Do you know it?

C: (*sings, looking directly at him*) You stop by, is it me you're here to see? You stop by, but have you any time for me?

(*pause*)

J: So you do know it?

C: Dawn breaking, but I never see. Stars shining, don't mean a thing to me. No time, no time. Busy drowning.

J: So that's what you were referring to?

C: No.

J: You don’t know anyone you think is drowning? You don’t feel like you’re drowning?

C: Everyone’s drowning.

J: Is that what you feel? We’re all drowning?

C: Aren’t we?

J: In what way?

C: We’re in over our heads. Everything’s falling apart and we’re looking for easy answers.

J: By we, you mean your generation?

C: No, yours. You created the mess.

J: You feel your generation has copped our mess?

C: Hasn’t it?

J: Somehow, I thought you might say that. (*He looks at his notes*)

C: Rabbits.

J: Sorry?

C: My favourite animal.

J: Oh. OK, great. Anything about them?

C: It was the first pet I ever had.

J: OK. Anything else?

C: No.

J: Are you sure?

C: Pandas.

J: Pandas? That's your second choice?

C: Because it was the first teddy bear I ever got.

J: OK, that it?

C: About pandas?

J: Yes.

C: They come from China.

J: Mmm-hmm.

C: And giraffes.

J: Any observations on giraffes?

C: I like Georgia the giraffe.

J: Is this a....who is Georgia?

C: She's in a programme called 64 Zoo Lane, on telly.

J: OK. Anything else you want to add?

C: You only asked for three.

J: No, I meant....any other observations on your choices? Why you chose them, what you feel about them, that sort of thing.

C: I've told you.

J: OK, well…

C: Is that the test?

J: Well, the animal you pick first is supposed to represent how you see yourself, which in your case is apparently....a rabbit. Because it was your first pet. The second choice was supposed to be how other people saw you.

C: A panda.

J: Yes, because that as your first teddy bear, and because they come from China.

C: Nice.

J: Whereas the final choice is supposed to represent who you really are.

C: Georgia the giraffe.

J: Quite.

C: It's very profound, isn't it?

J: Well, it doesn't always work.(silence)

C: Is that it with the animals?

J: Whilst googling your quote I also found a few references to the Raffel translation of Beowulf. Do you know what Beowulf is?

C: The poem?

J: (*nods*)

C: It's probably the oldest work of literature that we know of from Britain.

J: Very good. But that's not where the quote comes from, is it?

C: Did you check it?

J: Yes.

C: You read all of it?

J: Yes.

C: This is brilliant.

J: I'm glad you think so. I was up till about 2 o'clock in the morning finishing it.

C: Did you enjoy it?

J: Well, I was already familiar with it, though I'd never actually read it. I'll admit I'm glad it was the Raffel translation and not some Middle English affair.

C: Is the Raffel translation in modern English then?

J: Pretty much. Early 60s.

C: (*laughing*) I can't believe you sat up and read it all! That's so brilliant.

J: I'm glad to bring such joy into your life. So is the quote from someone you know?

C: No.

J: Really?

C: Yes.

J: So it is published?

C: That's how I found it.

J: Then why can't I google it?

C: Because I did something to stop you. Make you think a bit. Make you read Beowulf apparently.

J: How can you stop someone googling something?

C: There's a way.

J: There's a way. How?

C: (*shrugs*) Think about it.

J: (*sits staring at the table. After a few seconds she giggles*) You're loving this, aren't you?

C: Yes. But I'm not laughing at you, I promise.

J: Are you sure? I feel like a complete Charlie, scrabbling about in the dark here.

C: Perfect metaphor for life, don't you think?

J: So I can't google the quote because you've safeguarded it in some fashion. I can't understand the quote because you've chosen something totally arcane. And I can't understand your motives because you answer all my questions with questions. I don't get it. Please. Tell me. What's your rebellion? You seem to be pretty popular at school. You don't get bullied. You have no trouble with school work. Yet there's this constant swimming against the tide.

(*Heavy silence, during which he smiles as if something's occurred to him*)

J: Unless…

C: What?

J: Are you bored? Is that it? Is this simply because you're bored at school and think it's a waste of time?

C: No.

J: Are you sure? I mean you're obviously really bright You probably think the teachers have nothing they can tell you. Is that it?

C: No.

J: Then what is it? Come on, help me out here. At least answer a question with a question.

C: I'd need a question to answer then, wouldn't I?

J: You don't really need a question, do you?

C: (*little pause*) Would you like a foot massage?

J: (*longer pause*) No.

(*There's a heavy silence, in which Jacob writes in his notes, and Cleo looks back to looking at the framed qualifications on the 4th wall.*)

C: What's the English speaking union schools mace?

J: Sorry? Oh, it's a debating competition. Like an inter schools tournament.

C: Never heard of it.

J: Possibly not.

C: It's never come to our school. At least not since I've been there.

J: Well, I doubt your school's ever been entered.

C: But of course yours was. (shakes her head)

J: They are very different schools.

C: I'll bet they are. (*mutters under her breath*) Right of entitlement.

J: I'm sorry?

C: (*louder*) I said, right of entitlement.

J: Meaning?

(*Lighting takes on a distinct red tinge*)

C: Meaning you going to whatever school you went to put you in a completely different boat to me. A nice big comfy boat where you can sail happily off into the sunset, while people like me just get to wave you off, from the shore, with our dirty handkerchiefs. But should we have any problems, you'll be only too willing to sail back and sort us all out.

J: (*heavy silence*) Wow. So you...see yourself on a lower rung of the ladder to someone like myself?

C: Well I am, aren't I?

J: Do you feel let down?

C: More disappointed.

J: By your school?

C: By everything. Yes, my school, but what can they do? They just have to follow the rules like everybody else.

J: Would you say you were satisfied with the education you're get…

C: I'm not getting an education! None of us are! We're just being taught to pass exams. No more, no less. Like teaching monkeys to jump through hoops. It's all about where your school is in the league tables, like it's some kind of sport or something.

(*pause*)

J: And would you describe yourself as angry?

C: Would you?

J: We're discussing you. Do you see yourself as an angry person?

C: I see myself as a powerless person.

J: In what way powerless?

C: Because what will happen to me is completely predictable. We could sit here now and just map it all out.

J: So you feel trapped?

C: Let me think. Do I feel trapped by the trap? Yes.

J: What do you feel it would take to change this?

C: (*shrugs*) Right of entitlement?

J: What is, 'right of entitlement'? What does that mean?

C: What do you think it means?

J: Well, grammatically it doesn't mean anything. It's a complete tautology.

C: (*rolls her eyes*) And toy-tology is?

J: Tautology. It's...you know. When you say something twice.

C: Which I didn't.

J: Effectively you did, right and entitlement being the same thing. It's rather like saying a stream of water. What else would a stream be?

C: A stream of abuse?

J: OK. But context is everything. If I said I'd been swimming in a stream, you'd know instantly to what I was referring.

C: Even your language keeps me out. What's wrong with saying stream of water?

J: It's redundant.

C: You just said to me, "y'know....when you say something twice." Well, isn't 'y'know' redundant? And what about when people say things like, 'He turned around and said'. It doesn't mean anybody's spinning on the spot. It's just an expression. Surely the clue is in the word, expression. It's to help you express yourself. But somehow when I do that it becomes tautology?

J: Fair enough. Let's not get bogged down by this. So, right of entitlement refers to what? That the middle classes are more entitled than the working classes?

C: And they're not?

J: (*shakes head*) There's my girl. (*pause*)

C: Look, it's about confidence and a sense of entitlement. Things that are instilled at an early age. Society at large will rate you by how you rate yourself, so, present yourself as a success and very likely you'll be one. (*pause*)

J: How British do you feel?

C: What?

J: You said, even your language keeps me out. Just wondered if you felt British, Engish, Polish, or all three.

C: None, really.

J: So....essentially stateless.

C: I suppose.

J: OK. And is this something you embrace?

C: Being an outsider?

J: I didn't know if you saw it as having rebel status.

C: I'd always be an outsider on some level. If it's not where you're born, it's where you live, where you went to school, what you wear, who you know, or how you speak. We are blessed with our choice of cages.

J: And this bothers you, obviously.

C: Yes.

J: You feel you deserve a better future?

C: Why is it always about me? I'll survive whatever happens. But society's filled with those that won't, or can't, or simply don't know how to. Those not eloquent enough.

J: That isn't you. You're very eloquent.

C: Well there we are, I'll always have a gob on me. But there's plenty that haven't. Inarticulacy, a curse the middle classes know nothing about.(*Pause*)

J: What would you say if I said I could get you moved to a different school? One that might be capable of developing your abilities?

C: What...like grammar school?

J: What would you say?

C: Just me?

J: Yes. Just you.

C: And what would that solve?

J: How do you mean?

C: What would it change?

J: It would be a whole different experience for you.

C: For me, yes, but none of the others. (*Long silence*)

J: I see. So...you feel that would be, just, what, offering you a sop? A place in the same big boat as myself?

C: Well that's what it is, isn't it?

J: So the problem really is your view of society as a whole.

C: I can't expect you to understand. It's not your world.

(*Lights go down. Spotlight comes up, into which she walks.*)

C: (*To audience*) Being 11 years old is such a big thing, it's huge. You're coming out of childhood, but you're not a teenager yet, and up ahead, beyond that, lies maturity, or at least, you think it does. And there you are, between the stages, vulnerable and trusting. Then? Then along comes the 11+ and - POE! You're suddenly kicked one way or the other. It's all changed. You're now expected, at 11 years old, to know about...prime numbers and...verbal reasoning. But what if your parents don't know about these things? Yes of course schools are there to prepare you, if you're at private school that is, but regular schools? Down to your parents. And 90% of the time it's parental input that makes all the difference. So then...what happens if your parents work long hours? Because they didn't get much of an education either, but if they had, they very possibly could have shone. What then? Meanwhile, there are kids whose parents did get a good education, or can afford private tuition, who just sail through. Of course they do. Right of entitlement. But just for tonight, just for me, try to imagine how it feels when you've failed. How much it will affect your confidence, or your chances in life, or how it feels to actually meet those kids that pass. Are they aware of it? You bet they are. Then imagine how it feels to hear debates in which grammar schools are regularly described as being 'for the brightest kids'. "Why shouldn't the brightest kids have access to this opportunity?" people will say. And remember, this is just grammar schools. Beyond that there's private schools, and then public schools, where, as we all know too well, tomorrow's leaders will be taught confidence, ambition and right of entitlement.

(*Cleo turns and walks to the back of the stage. Jacob walks into the spotlight.*)

J: My parents were always very kind. Very understanding and supportive. Just, I don't know, a little remote I suppose. But that's the cliche, isn't it? With the better off, I mean. Pack em off to boarding school! Which my parents did in fact do. The school I went to wasn't all boarders, possibly 50:50. And it was a good school, though not especially prestigious. But it did have one claim to fame. Anthony Buckeridge. You know, the chap who wrote the Jennings books? He taught there. Long before my time, but he did show up one day to present a prize for design to my friend Tristram's brother. We were all thrilled I remember. Though the truth was I hadn't actually read the books. Have now. Big fan. (*pause*) Looking back, I suppose I did feel terribly pressurised, even though nothing was ever actually said. It was somehow in all the little gestures. It's odd really, because in exactly the same way, that's the dynamic I've created with Archie. Though I swore to myself I never would. Where Archie differs from me, though, is in his disapproval. I was pretty wet, I suppose. Not Archie. If he doesn't like something, he'll make his disapproval felt. Which is something he got from his mother. I could never do that. Always told myself I was too English. Too middle class, perhaps. But is it really that? Too English, or just too weak? Why is it so difficult to open up? To admit we need help? I mean, look at Cleo. She's fine with the soliloquies. But in real life she's...well, painting oblique quotes on a wall somewhere to express herself, and answering questions with questions.

(*Stage lights come up*)

C: Why don't you ask me more questions?

J: What would you like me to ask?

C: Would it make any difference if I told you?

J: Don't you want input into this?

C: What input could I possibly have?

J: Do you not think that's a little defeatist?

C: Defeatist, or defeated?

J: Don’t you know the difference?

C: Can’t you feel the inference?

J: Could I win your confidence?

(*Lights go down, spotlight comes up, and Cleo walks into it.*)

C: When I was little, my mother used to read to me. I don’t think I was all that comfortable with being unable to read, because I used to insist we sit at the kitchen table, opposite each other, like equals. I learnt to read quickly, and, before long, began reading for myself. But we, kind of, got used to doing it this way. So we carried on, sitting opposite each other, each reading our own thing in silence. My mother was a very good reader, it was she who taught me to read, in both Polish and English. So I thought it was odd when it dawned on me that, although she appeared to be reading, she hardly seemed to turn a page. One day I asked if she was actually reading, or using the time simply to think. No, she answered. I’m reading. At first I was confused, surely nobody could read that slowly, but gradually I began to realise what she was actually doing. She was truly reading, in other words, truly listening. Partaking, weighing each concept, considering the prose. We live in a time when people, if they read at all, don't often do that. Most of us just skim through social media, liking things without always even reading them, if we think we would agree, trying not to get our beliefs challenged. Taking from the tone instead of the content. Taking from the headlines and not the article. Seeing someone actually weighing the merits of a piece, or better still, reading for the sheer joy of doing so. That really impressed me.

(*Slowly the stage lights come up again.*)

J: Who are you talking to now? Me, or them? Is this part of the play?

C: I don't know. I don't know. What can you and I talk about? You don't see what upsets me. You think everything can be solved by getting into a better school, where I'd have a better chance of getting into a better university. Getting a better job and better money.

J: And that's not what you're looking for?

C: It’s not just a matter of getting into a good university, as if that were even an option for the kids at my school. They don’t have parents capable of playing the system, and our school sure in hell isn’t geared towards getting us into the Russell group universities. Besides, what is a good job? Have you got a good job? Has Archie?

J: Archie has his own business, designing websites.

C: Oh. So a non-job then?

J: How do you mean, a non-job?

C: Now who’s answering questions with questions? Is this Socratic?

J: I was just puzzled as to why Archie has a non-job.

C: I was being cruel. But it’s not really work, is it? I mean, designing websites. Bet he makes a killing on that. But if you have to actually work for a living, you know, driving a train or something, nursing people, delivering mail, whatever, then you’re on a set wage. His job’s a doddle.

J: You have to take into account the risk of the entrepreneur. Any new business may not take off. He could lose everything.

C: Has it ever once looked that way? And any skanky school kid can design a website. But it’s not about the doing, it’s about who you know. He’s got the contacts. Plus he’s got you and Susan to prop him up. And even if that all fell through, he could waitress.

J: Waitress?

C: You know, be a waiter. Or deliver pizzas or whatever. The kids at our school will only have that. It’s the only outcome for them. (*silence*)

J: Look, I admire your social conscience, I do, but the world is the world and always will be. You take the problems of the world on to your shoulders and they will bury you.

C: So what, we just do alright for ourselves, forget about anyone else?

J: Of course not!

C: Then why are our streets filled with homeless people? Why do so many people struggle to feed their kids? Or have to sleep in their cars cos rents are so high? Why has it become, in my lifetime, normal to see a food bank donation point in supermarkets?(*Jacob starts to pack up*)

J: I'm sorry, this is becoming propaganda now. Is that your intention, hmm? Plug for the Labour party? Well I'll tell you now, I'm not partaking. Happy now?

C: (*yells*) If I was happy would I have risked my bloody neck writing "Ruthless is clean unknowing the naked bones of heaven" on a sodding wall?(*exits*)

J: (*TA*) And there it was again, the truth. Here was a girl somehow able to infer a bigger picture from that which was available to her, and it had made her unhappy. But here's the thing, it wasn't about her. She was genuinely unhappy on behalf of other people. People she might be at school with. People she didn't know. People who may not even want to give her the time of day. It was incredible, really. Not something I'd encountered before.

J: After she died, Cleo was cremated in a very beautiful, very intimate ceremony, one July morning. But that was years later, God, she outlived me by about three decades.

(*Cleo enters.*)

C: I was quite a bit younger than you.

J: Well don't rub it in. (*He hands her an oven glove, which she dons, while similarly donning one himself.*)

J: You ready?

C: (*Holds up glove*)

Cleo had a little problem
What did she want to know?
For everywhere that Cleo went
That problem was sure to go.
It followed her to school, you know
Which was against the rule
The educational psychologist
He said…

J: (*Holds up glove*) You are no fool!
So I will send you to a school
That is a bit more posh
So all the things that worry you now
Will then seem so much tosh!

C: Thank you, said Cleo, for saving me
From drifting with the rest
So now I can join all of you.

J&C: The brightest and the best!